Let's Begin

LET'S GO

4th Edition

WORKBOOK

R. Nakata

K. Frazier

B. Hoskins

OXFORD
UNIVERSITY PRESS

Let's Talk

A Find Kate.

B Circle.

C Match.

1.   What's your name?

   I'm Scott.

2.   What's your name?

   I'm Kate.

3.   What's your name?

   I'm Jenny.

D Write ✓ or X.

1.  Stand up.

2.  Sit down.

Let's Learn

A Match.

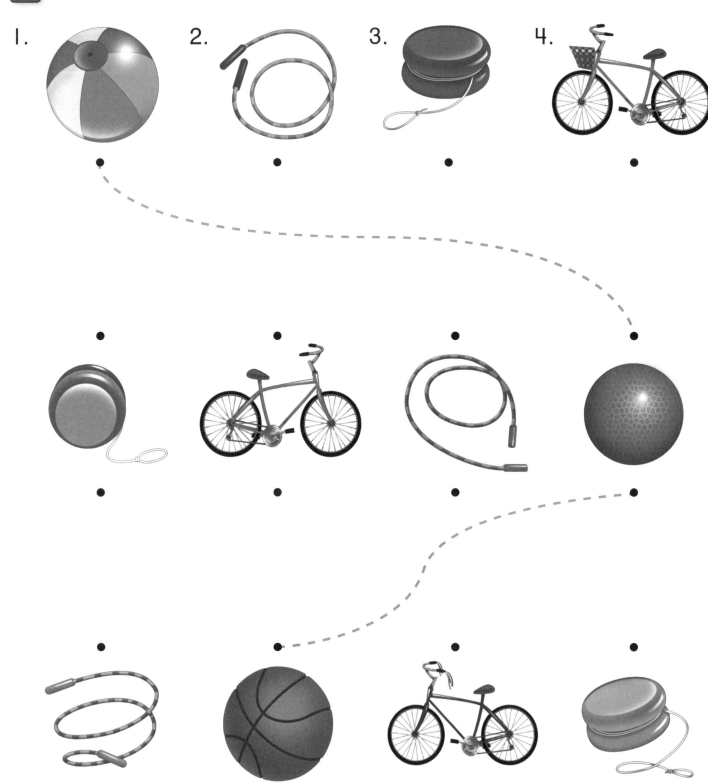

1.

2.

3.

4.

B Trace, find, and circle.

It's a ball.

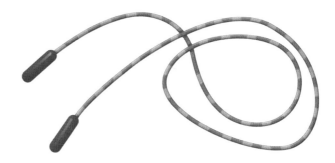

It's a jump rope.

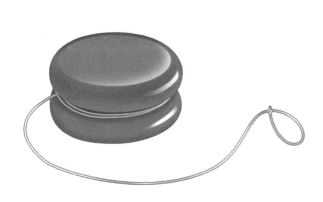

It's a yo-yo.

It's a bicycle.

Let's Learn More

A Trace and color.

a train

a doll

a car

a teddy bear

B Match.

1. It's a train.

2. It's a car.

3. It's a doll.

4. It's a teddy bear.

C Match and say.

What is it?

It's a _____.

1.

2.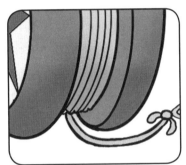

3.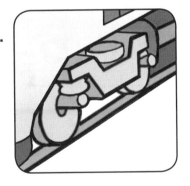

4.

Phonics

A Connect.

Aa   Cc   Ee

Ii   Dd   Ff

Bb   Hh   Gg

Jj   Mm   Nn   Oo

Kk   Ss   Pp

Ll   Tt   Qq

Vv   Uu   Rr

Ww   Xx   Yy   Zz

B Trace and write.

What's your name?

1. **I'm Andy.** Andy
2. **I'm Jenny.** Jenny
3. I'm _____ . Kate
4. I'm _____ . Scott

C Write your name. Draw a picture.

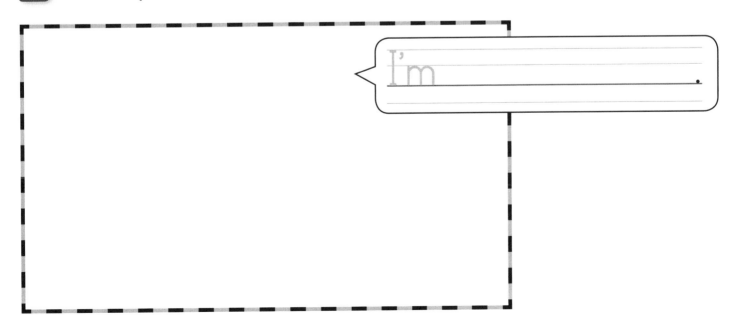

I'm _____ .

Let's Talk

A Find.

B Match and say.

1.

2.

C Write ✓ or X.

1.

Come here.

 X

 ✓

2.

Turn around.

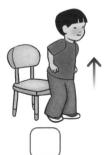

Let's Learn

A Match and color.

1. red

2. blue

3. yellow

4. green

5. brown

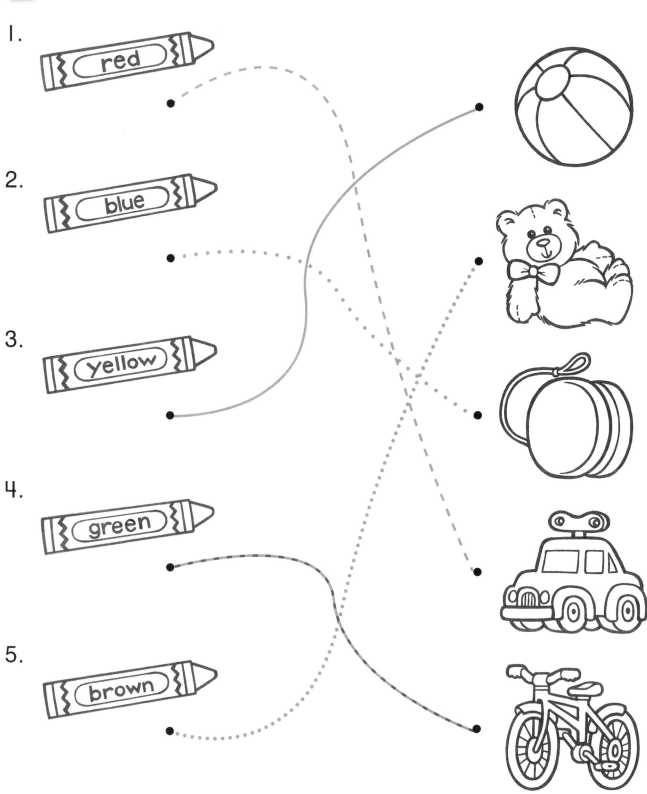

B Trace and color.

1.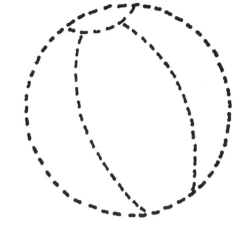

It's [red] .

2.

It's [blue] .

3.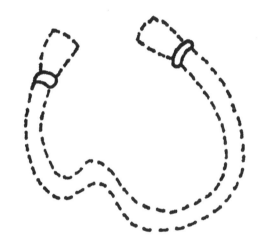

It's [green] .

4.

It's [yellow] .

5.

It's [brown] .

A Color and write.

1.

It's white.

It's _____.

2.

It's orange.

It's _____.

3.

It's purple.

It's _____.

4.

It's pink.

It's _____.

5.

It's black.

It's _____.

B Find and color.

What color is it?

It's red.   It's purple.   It's orange.   It's brown.   It's black.

Let's Learn to Read

Phonics

A Circle and say.

1. **A**	2. **B**	3. **C**	4. **D**
c	B	A	a
(a)	d	c	c
(A)	a	d	D
D	C	C	B
B	b	C	c

B Match.

1.  •

2.  •

3.  •

4.   •

 • •

  • •

 • •

 •

 a •

 b •

 c •

 d •

C Trace and write.

1. What is it?

2. It's a yo-yo.

3. It's a ball.

4. It's a train.

5. What is it?

6. It's a _____ .

7. It's a _____ .

8. It's a _____ .

Parent's
signature: _____

Let's Review ✓

A Circle.

1. It's a jump rope.

2. It's a doll.

3. It's blue.

4. It's purple.

B Match.

1.

Come here.

2.

Stand up.

3.

Sit down.

4.

Turn around.

School Supplies

A Match and trace.

1.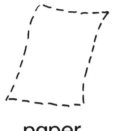

   paper

2.

   scissors

3.

   glue

4.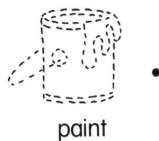

   paint

5.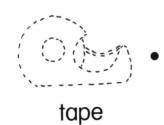

   tape

I have scissors.

I have paint.

I have paper.

I have tape.

I have glue.

Let's Talk

A Match.

1.

How are you today?

I'm fine.

2.

How are you today?

I'm fine, thanks.

3.

How are you today?

I'm fine, thank you.

B Write ✓ or X.

1.

Walk.

X ✓ ☐

2.

Run.

☐ ☐ ☐

C Match and say.

Stand up. Walk. Turn around. Run. Sit down.
• • • • •

Let's Learn

A Trace.

1.

a circle

2.
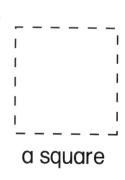
a square

3.
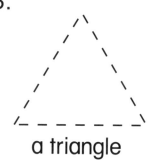
a triangle

4.
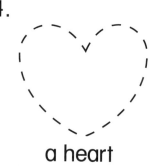
a heart

B Complete the pattern.

1.

2.

3.
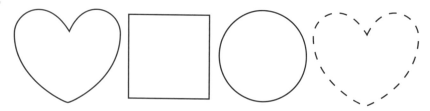

C Trace. Then draw.

1. Draw a circle.

2. Draw a triangle.

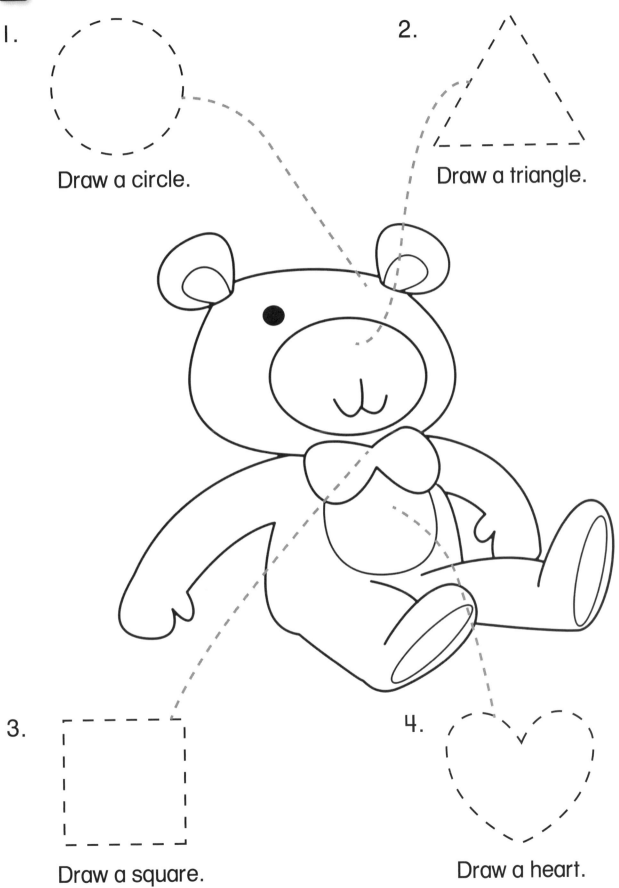

3. Draw a square.

4. Draw a heart.

A Match and circle.

1.
   a star

2.
   a rectangle

3.
   a diamond

4.
   an oval

B Trace.

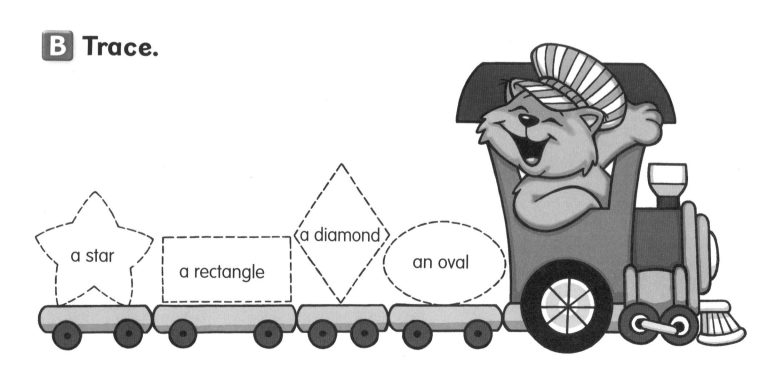

a star

a rectangle

a diamond

an oval

C Complete the pattern. Write.

1. Is it a star?

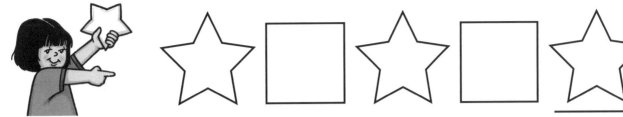

Yes, it is.

2. Is it an oval?

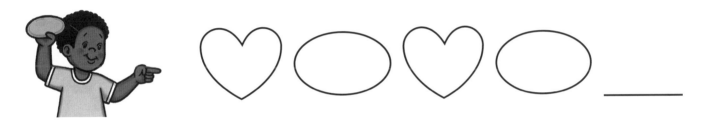

No, it isn't. It's a heart.

3. Is it a triangle?

_____ .

Let's Learn to Read

Phonics

A Circle and say.

1. **EFGH**

   abcd
   (EFGH)
   BCDE
   cdef
   EFGH

2. **efgh**

   defg
   efgh
   DEFG
   efgh
   CDEF

B Circle and trace.

1.

2.

3.

4.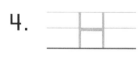

C Trace and write.

1. Is it a star?

   Yes, it is.

a star

2. Is it a rectangle?

   No, it isn't.

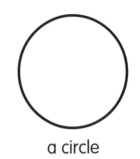

a circle

3. Is it an oval?

   Yes, _____.

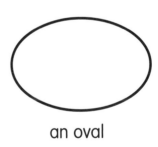

an oval

4. Is it a triangle?

   No, _____.

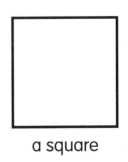

a square

A Match or *X*.

1.

2.

May I come in?

Sure! Please come in!

3.

5.

4.

A Trace.

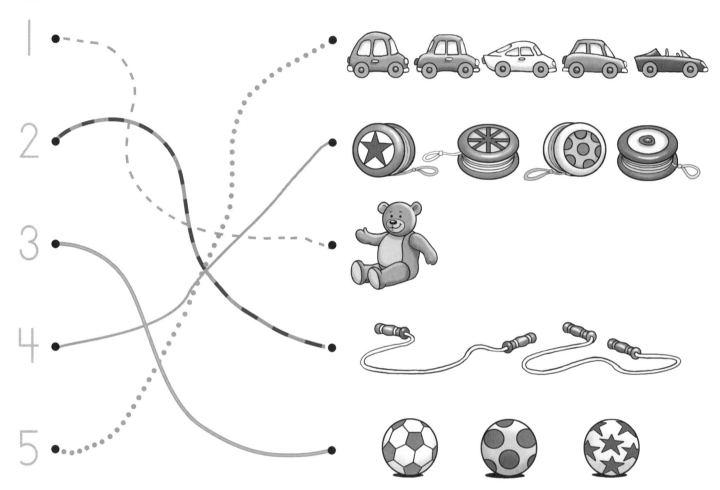

B Color.

1. 3

2. 5

3. 4

4. 2

C Draw and say.

Let's Learn More

A Trace and match.

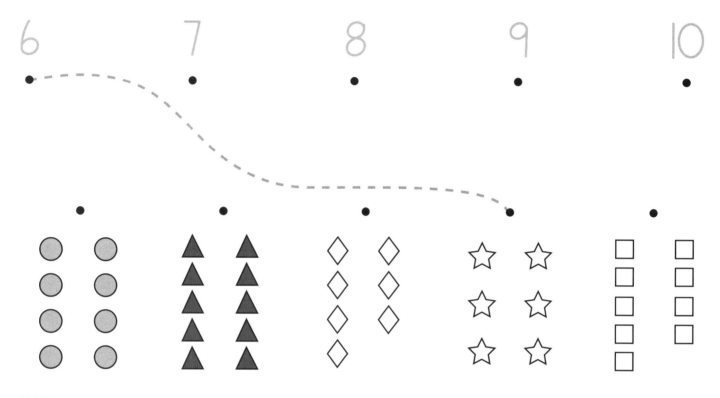

6   7   8   9   10

B Write ✓ or X.

1. **7**

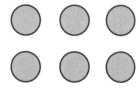

2. **10**

C Count and write.

1. How many?

6

2. How many?

___

3. How _____ ?

___

4. _____ ?

___

Let's Learn to Read

Phonics

A Draw.

I i = △   J j = ◯   K k = ☐   L l = ♡

I   J   L   E   k   L   K
c   a   F   B
I   i   l   j   k   i   d
f   k   I   h   A   b
K   H   I   j   D   J

B Match and trace.

1. I •   •  •   • i

2. J •    • j

3. K •   •  •   • k

4. L •   •  •   • l

C Match and write.

1.
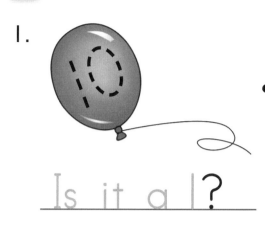

Is it a 1?

Yes, it is.

2.

Is it a 2?

No, it isn't.

_____

3.

Is it a 9?

_____

Let's Review ✓

A Find and circle.

1.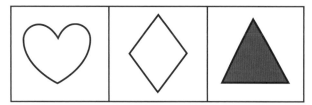

2.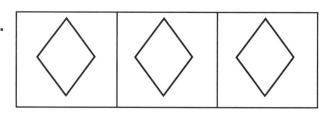

3.

4.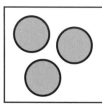

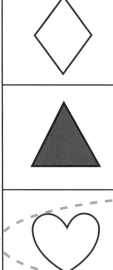    

Classroom Commands

A Circle.

1. Take out your pencil.

2. Close your book.

3. Open your book.

4. Put away your pencil.

Let's Talk

A Match.

Here you are.

Thank you.

Here you are.

Thank you.

Here you are.

Thank you.

B Match and say.

1.

Jump.

2.

Skip.

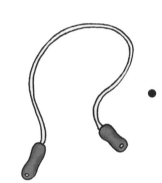

C Write ✓ or X.

1.

Skip.

2.

Jump.

Let's Learn

A Number.

1.

bird

2.

cat

3.

dog

4.

birds

5.

cats

6.

dogs

B How many? Write and say.

1.

3 cats

2.

bird

3.

dogs

4.

dog

5.

cat

6.

birds

✓ Parent's
signature: _____

Unit 5 Animals   **41**

Let's Learn More

A Find.

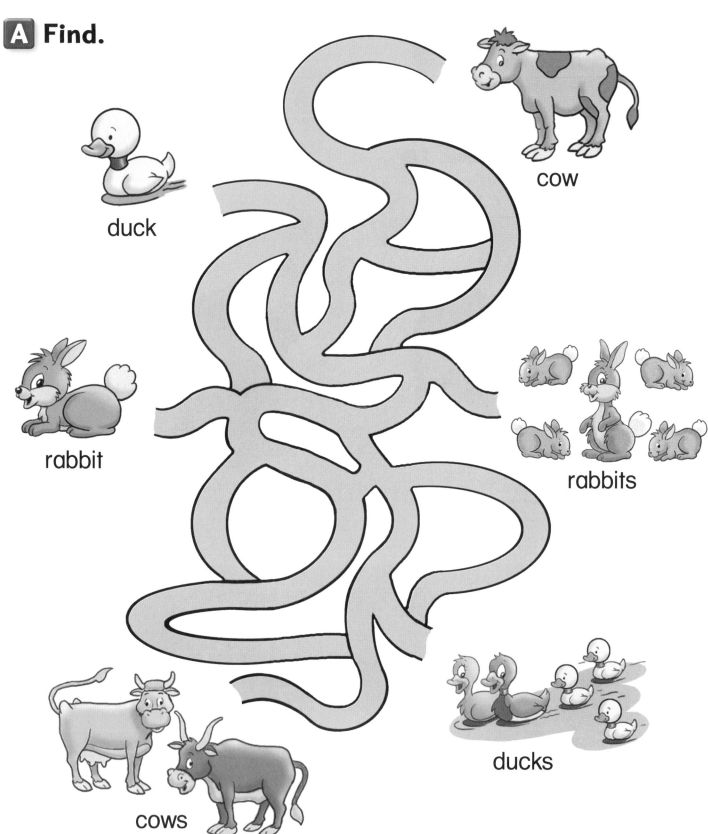

duck

cow

rabbit

rabbits

cows

ducks

B Count and write.

1. How many cows? _____ cows.

2. How many ducks? _____ ducks.

3. How many dogs? _____ dog.

4. How many birds? _____ birds.

5. How many rabbits? _____ rabbits.

Let's Learn to Read

A Find and circle.

Phonics

A	M	N	O	P	A	m	n	o	p
C	a	L	b	o	p	K	j	i	M
m	N	O	D	M	N	O	P	h	n
n	m	n	o	p	g	m	n	o	p
M	N	O	P	f	E	n	F	I	B
N	H	P	m	n	o	p	G	P	k
p	c	I	d	e	M	N	O	P	J

B Trace and match.

1. Mm •

2. Nn •

3. Oo •

4. Pp •

C Match, and say. Count and write.

1.

How many dolls?

cars

2.

How many cars?

3.

How many balls?

3 dolls

Let's Talk

A Draw.

How old are you?

1. I'm 6.

2. I'm 8.

3. I'm 5.

4. I'm 10.

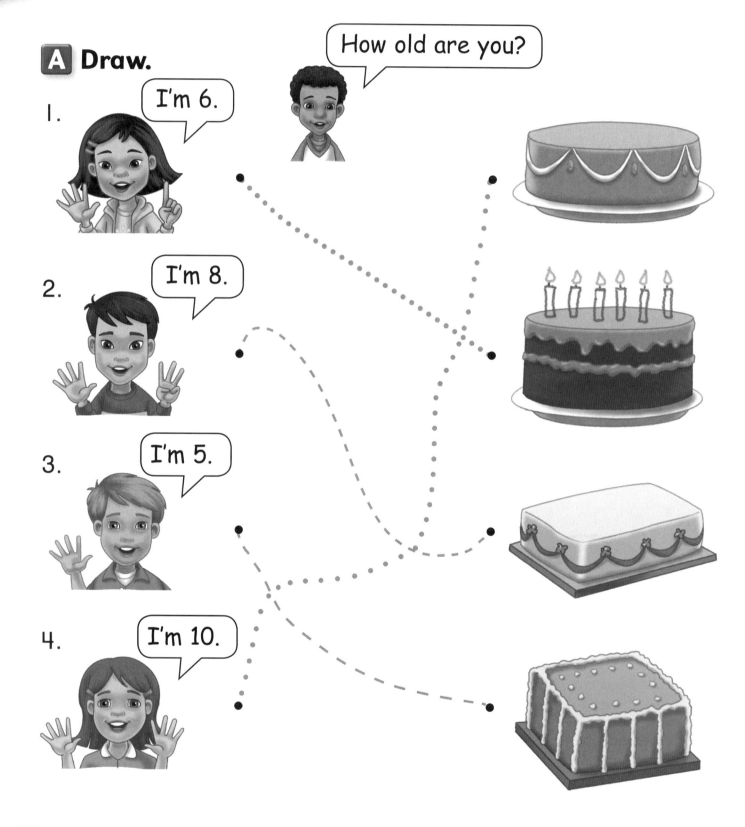

B How old are you? Draw and color.

C Write ✓ or X.

1.

Make a line.

 X   ✓

2.

Make a circle.

Let's Learn

A Match

1.

2.

3.

4.

ice cream

pizza

cake

chicken

B Write and number.

1.

I like ice cream.

2.

I like chicken.

3.

I like _____.

4.

I like _____.

Let's Learn More

A Circle.

1.

milk

2.

rice

3.

bread

4.

fish

B Find.

1. Do you like rice?
   Yes, I do.

2. Do you like fish?
   No, I don't.

3. Do you like milk?
   Yes, I do.

4. Do you like bread?
   No, I don't.

Let's Learn to Read

Phonics

A Write ✓ or X.

1. Q R S T   F G H I   Q R S T   O P Q R
                 X   ✓   ☐

2. q r s t   d e f g   p q r s   q r s t
              ☐   ☐   ☐

3. Q r s T   Q R S T   q R s T   Q r s T
              ☐   ☐   ☐

B Match and trace.

1. Q

2. R   sun   tiger

3. S

4. T   rabbit   queen

C Write and say.

1. <u>Do you like cake?</u>

<u>Yes, I do.</u>

<u>No, I don't.</u>

2. <u>Do you like pizza?</u>

<u>Yes,   .</u>

3. <u>Do you like fish?</u>

<u>No,   .</u>

4. <u>Do you like   ?</u>

<u>   .</u>

Let's Review ✓

A Match.

1.

2.

3.

4.

5.

6.

4 cats

ice cream

rice

1 rabbit

skip

make a circle

The Weather

A **Match and trace.**

1.
sunny

2.
cloudy

3.
windy

4.
rainy

5.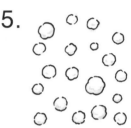
snowy

It's rainy.

It's cloudy

It's sunny.

It's windy.

It's snowy.

Let's Talk

A Match.

1.

Oops! I'm sorry.

That's OK.

2.

Oops! I'm sorry.

That's OK.

3.

Oops! I'm sorry.

That's OK.

B Match.

Clap your hands.

Stamp your feet.

1.

2.

3.

4.

5.

C Number.

1.

Sit down.

2.

Jump.

3.

Run.

4.

Skip.

5.

Walk.

Let's Learn

A Circle.

1.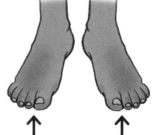

head

2.

shoulders

3.

knees

4.

toes

B Match.

1.

I can touch my knees.

2.

I can touch my shoulders.

3.

I can touch my head.

4.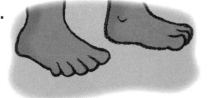

I can touch my toes.

Let's Learn More

A Match.

1.  2.  3.  4.

B Draw.

eyes

mouth

ears

nose

C Number and write.

What can you do?

1.

2.

3.

4.

I can touch my ears.

I can touch my _____ .

I can touch _____ .

I can _____ .

Phonics

A Circle and say.

1. U

2. V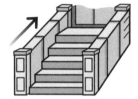

3. W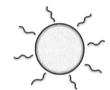

B Match and trace.

1.

2.

3.

C Write and say.

1. What can you do?
   I can touch my toes.

2. What can you do?
   I can clap my hands.

3. What can you do?
   I can run.

4. What can you do?
   I can jump.

✓ Parent's
signature: _____

Let's Talk

A Find.

Let's play.

OK. Let's play tag.

Let's play.

OK. Let's jump rope.

B Trace.

1.

Point to the board.

2.

Go to the board.

C Write ✓ or X.

1.

Go to the board.

X

✓

☐

2.

Point to the board.

☐

☐

☐

Let's Learn

A Match.

1.

2.

3.

4.

fly a kite

sing a song

bounce a ball

ride a bicycle

B Match and say.

I can . . .   I can't . . .

1.

2.

3.

4.

Let's Learn More

A Find and circle.

 wink

 smile

 swim

 dance

B Write and say.

Can you dance?

Yes, I can.   No, I can't.

1. Can you sing?

Yes, _____.

2. Can you wink?

No, _____.

3. Can you smile?

_____.

Let's Learn to Read

Phonics

A Draw.

X x = ◆   Y y = ⬭   Z z = ▬

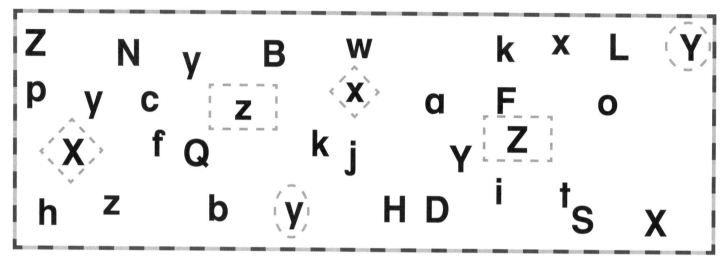

Z   N   y   B   w   k   x   L   Y

p   y   c   z   X   a   F   o

X   f Q   k j   Y   Z

h   z   b   y   H D   i   t S   X

B Circle and trace.

1. ╳          fox

2. Y       yarn

3. Z        zebra

C Write and say.

1. I can wink.

2. I can't swim.

3. I can smile.

4. I can't ride a bike.

5. bounce a ball.

6. dance.

A Find and number.

1

2

3

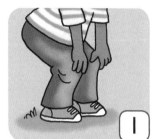
4

5

6

7

8

Days of the Week

A Match.

Sunday	Monday	Tuesday	Wednesday	Thursday	Friday	Saturday
1	2	3	4	5	6	7

Alphabet Practice

A Color and trace.

bird

apple →

dog ↓

cat →

A a B b C c D d

B **Color and trace.**

heart →

gorilla →

egg

fish ↑

E E e F F f G G g H H h

C Color and trace.

igloo →

kangaroo →

lion ←

jump rope ←

Ii Jj Kk Ll

D Color and trace.

moon

nest

octopus

panda

M m N n O o P p

E Color and trace.

sun →

queen ←

↑ rabbit

tiger ↓

Q q q R r r S s s T t

F **Color and trace.**

umbrella →

violin →

watch ←

G Color and trace.

yarn

zebra

fox

X x   Y y   Z z